Reflections on
SISTERHOOD

Voices from Black Canada

By:

- ▶ Pauline Taylor-Bloomfield
- ▶ Hermia Morton Anthony
- ▶ Asali Quamina
- ▶ Murphy Browne
- ▶ Audra Townsend
- ▶ Helen Pearman Ziral
- ▶ Rita Burke
- ▶ Herma Killingbeck
- ▶ Nancy Fraser

Compiled and published by: Burke's Publishing

Table Of Contents

Foreword

As the daughter of Rita—one of seven sisters who has long understood the power of Sisterhood—I have witnessed these connections firsthand, watching my mother and aunties move through life together. I am a girlchild, the youngest of two, with an older brother but no blood sisters. Fortunately, my bonds with my cousins and the women from my elementary, high school, and university years have shown me the depth and significance of sisterhood.

Though I am not a member of a Black sorority, my time at Spelman College deepened my appreciation for sisterhood and kinship—something I practice daily. As an adult, a business owner, and a Black woman navigating spaces that often seek to define us before we define ourselves, I know that sisterhood is both refuge and revolution.

Sisterhood is seen and unspoken, shaping our lives in ways we may not always recognize. It is whispered in childhood confidences, echoed in the laughter of chosen family, and reaffirmed in the quiet moments when words are unnecessary. It is a bond formed through experience, strengthened by resilience, and held together by the shared understanding of what it means to navigate this world as a Black woman.

The essays, poems, and reflections in Reflections on Sisterhood: Voices from Black Canada move in a rhythm that mirrors how Sisterhood weaves through our lives. Each piece offers a unique perspective on this unbreakable bond. Some speak of sisterhood as an inheritance passed down through generations—something to be honoured and upheld. Others remind us that sisterhood is not always freely given; sometimes, it must be sought, built, and even fought for. Layered and distinct voices come together in a shared truth: sisterhood evolves alongside the women who embody it.

Pauline opens this collection with a poem that celebrates sisterhood as a bond that endures life's joys and hardships, steadfast across time and distance.

Hermia reminds us that sisterhood begins in childhood, where biological sisters become the first mirror we see of ourselves, shaping the following relationships.

Asali highlights the power of authenticity—when we model vulnerability and openness, we create space for younger women to embrace their truths.

Murphy underscores the deep connections built on love, trust, and understanding. At the same time, Audra challenges us to examine the boundaries of sisterhood—who defines them and who has historically been welcomed within them.

Helen affirms that sisterhood is more than friendship; it is an unbreakable bond woven with compassion, empathy, and mutual respect.

Rita transports us to a time when learning from elders was not only expected but revered, showing how sisterhood often carries the wisdom of generations.

Herma brings this intergenerational bond to life through Miss Patsy, whose warmth and wisdom are shared through words and food, nurturing a sense of belonging.

Nancy closes the collection with a reflection on modern sisterhood in digital spaces—where a hashtag can feel like an embrace, a lifeline of solidarity across screens.

This collection affirms that sisterhood is more than blood. It exists in the friends who become family, the elders who take us in, the mentors who guide us, and the communities that hold us when the world threatens to pull us apart.

This anthology does not seek to define sisterhood singularly but instead offers a chorus of voices, each adding depth to our collective experience—including my own. It is a reflection of love, growth, and the ways we hold one another up.

Whether you come to this collection seeking recognition, comfort, or a deeper understanding of what sisterhood means to you, may these stories remind you of one thing: you are not alone.

- Leah

Of blood and kin I thee celebrate. The journey of love and friendship that we have been bonded throughout life's ups and downs.

Pauline Taylor-Bloomfield

.... ━━━━━━━━━━━━ ....

Pauline Taylor-Bloomfield is a retired elementary school teacher. She enjoys travelling and writing. She is the author of the book What M a k e s The World Beautiful, which is her first published work for children. She also writes and recites poetry. Pauline is grateful to have five sisters in her family and numerous other sister-friends who have encouraged, supported, influenced and cheered her on throughout her life's journey.

From childhood to the present, sisters are an essential part of her village, nurturing her soul and expanding her horizons

.... ━━━━━━━━━━━━ ....

1

I KNOW HER

Of blood and kin I thee celebrate
The journey of love and friendship
That we've been on
Kindred spirits bonded
Throughout life's ups and downs
Forever holding dear the essence
Of our shared humanity.

You span many years of my life
Planting seeds that blossom
And envelop us
Growing into a symbiotic relationship
Of love and respect that nurtures the soul.

I know your kind and gentle ways
And the echoes and yearnings of your heart

I know the beautiful soul you possess
And share with others.

I know the depth of your thinking
And your endeavour to create and learn
I know the emotional being you are
And watch you share your love with others.
I know your hopes and dreams
And the work you do to make them a reality
I know your nurturing, giving spirit
And the myriad of ways you help and uplift
others.

I know your laughter and your joy
Shared so wholesomely with the world
I know the heaviness of your heart
When others hurt, or you are hurt.
I know you value life and all things good
By the life you live and the thankful prayers
You lift to the Creator.

I know you draw strength from within
And let others in when needed
I know that you cherish life
And those God has placed within yours.

I know your goal is to do no harm to others
And to do all the good you can in this our world.
I know that my life is richer
For having you in it
I know that you are beautiful inside and out

And in that, I rest assured
That I have found a friend and a SISTER
for life!

The foundations of Sisterhood are laid during childhood, where sisters share a significant portion of their early lives.

Hermia Morton Anthony

Hermia Morton Anthony, a sister, womanist, social justice activist, community organizer, and educator, is a unique blend of Kittitian/Liamiguan heritage and African ancestry. Her pioneering publications shed new light on women and Black and Indigenous populations in the Caribbean and North America. Her latest work, Women in the St. Kitts Island Uprising, released in 2025, is a testament to her unwavering commitment to sharing empowering narratives from women. The audience can appreciate and support her significant contributions to community and empowerment.

2

THE COMPLEXITIES OF SISTERHOOD

Sisterhood, a relationship formed by sisters, is a multifaceted and profoundly intricate bond shaped by various socio-cultural, psychological, and personal factors. It represents and transcends biological ties between women and girls. Unlike other relationships, a sisterhood encompasses a unique blend of shared experiences, emotional connections, rivalries, and mutual support. Women frequently view the complexities accompanying sisterhood bonding through different lenses, such as childhood experiences, adolescence, adulthood, cultural influences, collective commitments, and individual personalities. In this article, we will delve into these aspects to understand a sisterhood's profound and often paradoxical nature.

▶ Girlhood

The foundations of a sisterhood are laid during childhood when biological sisters share a significant portion of their early lives. This period is marked by numerous shared experiences, from playing and learning together to facing challenges and celebrating milestones. Childhood memories, whether filled with joy or conflict, form the bedrock of the sisterly bond.

Sisters often develop a sense of companionship and solidarity during this time. They learn to navigate family dynamics and understand each other's personalities to create a unique communication style. However, childhood is also a period of competition for parental attention and resources, which can lead to sibling rivalry. This rivalry, often perceived negatively, can foster a sense of determination and resilience in sisters, inspiring growth even in conflict.

▶ Adolescence

Adolescence is a transformative phase in a person's life and brings new dimensions to the sisterly relationship. As sisters navigate the complexities of growing up, they provide each other with emotional support, guidance, and a sense of belonging. The shared journey through the turbulent teenage years can strengthen their bond as they confide in each other about their fears, aspirations, and experiences.

However, adolescence is also a time when sisters strive to establish their identities separate from their families. This quest for independence can sometimes lead to conflicts, as sisters may have differing opinions, interests, and social circles.

Despite these challenges, the bond often prevails as sisters learn to respect each other's individuality while maintaining their connection.

▶ Adulthood

As sisters transition into adulthood, their relationships continue to evolve. The responsibilities and challenges of adult life, such as career choices, parenthood, and marriage, add new layers to their bond. Sisters often become pillars of support for each other, offering advice, empathy, and a sense of continuity.

Geographic distance, life circumstances, and personal growth can influence the dynamics of the sisterly relationship in adulthood. While some sisters may maintain a close and consistent relationship, others may experience periods of estrangement and reconnection. The ability to navigate these fluctuations with understanding and compassion is a testament to the resilience of the sisterly bond.

▶ Cultural Influences

Culture plays a significant role in shaping the nature of sisterhood. Different cultures have varying expectations and norms regarding familial relationships, influencing how sisters interact. In some cultures, sisters maintain close-knit relationships and provide lifelong support, while other cultures value individual independence.

Cultural rituals, traditions, and societal expectations can also impact the dynamics of sisterhood. For example, in some cultures, sisters play a crucial role in family ceremonies and celebrations, reinforcing their bond through shared responsibilities and experiences. Understanding the cultural context is essential to appreciate the nuances and variations in sisterly relationships across different societies.

▶ Emotional and Psychological Dimensions

The emotional and psychological aspects of a sisterhood are deeply intertwined. Sisters often serve as confidantes, sounding boards, and sources of emotional support. The shared history and intimate knowledge of each other's lives create a unique emotional connection that can provide comfort and validation.

However, the emotional closeness can also lead to conflicts and misunderstandings. The intensity of the relationship means disagreements are often unresolved because issues from the past can resurface. Effective communication, empathy, and conflict resolution skills, which are crucial in maintaining a healthy, balanced, sisterly relationship, can help in these situations.

▶ Individual Personalities

The individual personalities of sisters play a significant role in shaping the dynamics of their relationship. Each sister brings her own set of traits, strengths, weaknesses, and perspectives to the bond. These individual differences can complement each other, creating a harmonious and enriching relationship or clash, leading to conflicts and tensions.

For example, a more extroverted sister might encourage her introverted sibling to step out of her comfort zone, fostering personal growth. Conversely, differing temperaments and communication styles can lead to misunderstandings and friction. Recognising and appreciating each other's unique qualities is essential in nurturing a positive sisterly relationship.

▶ The Impact of Life Transitions

Life transitions, such as marriage, parenthood, career changes, and aging, can significantly impact the dynamics of a sisterhood. These transitions often bring new responsibilities, challenges, and growth opportunities. Sisters can provide invaluable support during these times by offering practical help, emotional encouragement, and a sense of continuity.

In particular, marriage and parenthood can bring joy and complexity to the bond. Adding new family members and the demands of caregiving can shift priorities and require adjustments in the relationship. Sisters may need to navigate new roles, boundaries, and expectations while maintaining their connection.

▶ The Role of Shared Experiences

Shared experiences are a cornerstone of a sisterhood, creating a repository of memories and moments that define relationships. These experiences range from significant life events like family vacations and holidays to everyday interactions and inside jokes. The shared history provides a sense of continuity and belonging, reinforcing the bond between sisters and reminding them of the strength of their shared history.

However, the weight of shared experiences can also be a source of tension. Past conflicts, unresolved issues, and differing perceptions of events can create friction and distance. Reflecting on and reconciling these experiences with empathy and understanding is crucial in maintaining a healthy and supportive sisterly relationship.

▶ Sisterhood in the Digital Age

Sisterhood in the digital age refers to online connections, communities, and relationships among women. Women from diverse backgrounds and locations can connect globally, share experiences, support one another, and celebrate milestones and successes. In addition, factors such as technology and social media often influence the dynamics of a sisterhood. The advent of digital communication has made it easier for sisters to stay connected, regardless of geographical distance. However, social media platforms also can be detrimental to users who may face online harassment. Challenges include the potential for miscommunication and the pressure of maintaining an idealised image online. Sisters must navigate these complexities with awareness to ensure their relationships remain authentic and grounded.

By acknowledging both the benefits and challenges of Sisterhood in the digital age, women can work towards creating a more inclusive, supportive, and empowering online community to foster the sisterhood. Digital spaces offer the opportunity to strengthen the bonds of sisterhood.

▶ Conclusion

The complexity of a sisterhood reflects the intricate and multifaceted nature of human relationships. From childhood to adulthood, cultural influences to individual personalities, the bond between sisters is shaped by many factors that create a rich and dynamic tapestry of experiences.

Sisterhood encompasses a unique blend of companionship, support, and conflict. It is a relationship marked by deep emotional connections, shared history, and the capacity for mutual growth. Despite the challenges and fluctuations, the resilience and enduring nature of sisterly bonds will highlight the profound impact of this relationship on an individual's life.

By understanding the complexities of sisterhood, we gain a deeper appreciation for the women and girls and navigate their unique journeys together, offering each other love, challenges, support, criticism, and a sense of unparalleled belonging. The sisterly bond is a testament to the strength and beauty of female bonding, reminding us of the enduring power of connection and the profound influence of those who share our lives.

When we model our openness for younger women, we demonstrate that true strength lies in authenticity.

Asali Quamina

Asali Quamina is a seasoned leader, educator, and advocate for childcare and women's empowerment. For over 25 years, she has been the executive director of a nonprofit childcare center, where she has dedicated her life to creating supportive spaces for growth and learning. Her commitment to empowering teenage mothers, providing guidance and resources to help them navigate parenthood and achieve their goals, is a source of inspiration and hope for her audience. She has developed innovative programs and initiatives specifically tailored to the needs of these young mothers, addressing the unique challenges they face and helping them build a better future for themselves and their children.

As an educator, Asali inspired countless students during her 12 years teaching the Childcare Assistant Program with the Toronto District School Board, shaping the next generation of childcare professionals. Beyond her professional endeavors, she has organized transformative retreats and workshops, fostering connection, healing, and empowerment for women in her community.

A proud wife, mother, grandmother, and great-grandmother, Asali draws on her wealth of personal and professional experiences to champion the values of family, community, and compassion as keys to creating lasting change.

3

SISTERHOOD AS A LEGACY

How the Bonds We Create Shape the Future

Sisterhood as a Legacy emphasises how the bonds of sisterhood create lasting impacts across generations. This chapter will examine the values, lessons, and traditions passed down between women and how nurturing these bonds can shape not only individuals but an entire generation, fostering lasting support, resilience, and love.

Sisterhood is more than a relationship; it is a tradition, a collection of shared stories, values, and lessons passed down through generations. Women who support, uplift, and inspire each other establish an enduring legacy of love, resilience, and solidarity. The strength we find in our sisters—biological or chosen—becomes a beacon toward kindness, courage, and self-discovery.

This chapter explores how sisterhood influences those around us, from daughters and nieces to young women in our communities. Through personal stories and insights, we will examine how passing down the spirit of sisterhood nurtures strong, supportive bonds that echo through time.

▶ The Foundation Of Sisterhood: Lessons From Those Who Came Before Us:

Every generation learns from the one before, whether we realise it or not. Many of us have inherited wisdom and strength from the women who raised us—mothers, grandmothers, aunts, or older sisters. These women become our first examples of what sisterhood can look like. Their stories, both told and untold, shape our beliefs about friendship, support, and the strength found in female bonds.

For example, Maria recalls the close bond between her mother and her aunts. Growing up, she watched them navigate hardships with a unified front, showing her that sisterhood is about loyalty and resilience. These role models taught her that having someone by your side can make all the difference, even when life presents challenges. Now, as an adult, she carries their lessons forward, nurturing bonds with her friends and cousins in the same spirit.

Through these examples, we see how sisterhood is often a learned behaviour. The values passed down—loyalty, empathy, and unwavering support—become the building blocks for the relationships we create. By recognising and sharing these lessons, we continue the legacy, empowering younger generations to build their supportive bonds.

▶ Passing Down Traditions And Rituals

Traditions, whether small or grand, play a significant role in sustaining the bonds of sisterhood across generations. These shared practices create continuity, connecting us to the women who came before us and those who will follow. Some traditions might be family-oriented, like gathering for annual sister "reunions," while others may be smaller, personal rituals, like sharing letters or notes of encouragement.

Example: Anna and her three sisters share a unique tradition: every year, on each sister's birthday, they each write a note of appreciation highlighting the past year's growth, achievements, and funny memories. This tradition passed from their grandmother, who believed in the power of kind words to uplift each other. Now, as adults, they cherish these notes as reminders of their bond, creating a collective history that they hope to pass on to their daughters.

Through such rituals, we demonstrate to future generations the importance of celebrating each other. These small but meaningful practices can encourage younger women to create similar traditions with their friends and loved ones, cementing the value of sisterhood in their lives.

▶ The Role Of Sisterhood In Shaping Self-Worth And Confidence

Sisterhood often plays a profound role in building self-confidence and teaching us to value ourselves. Sisters become our first champions by offering unconditional support and encouragement, helping us recognise our unique strengths. This support can impact self-esteem, shaping how we view ourselves and interact with the world.

Consider Emma and her niece, Sophie. Emma, a single aunt, stepped into a guiding role when Sophie's mother passed away. As Sophie navigated her teenage years, Emma was there for her, encouraging her dreams and helping her overcome self-doubt. She encouraged Sophie to explore her creativity and reminded her of her worth when insecurities crept in. Emma became Sophie's role model and mentor, proving that sisterhood is not limited to peers. Emma and Sophie showed that the bond formed and nurtured exists between generations.

By teaching young women to value themselves, we extend the legacy of sisterhood, instilling a self-esteem they can pass on to others. This confidence enables future generations to lift each other and celebrate their unique qualities.

▶ Modelling Resilience And Adaptability

Life often presents challenges, from personal hardships to career obstacles. How we respond to these situations can teach invaluable lessons about resilience, adaptability, and the importance of having a support network. When women model resilience for each other, they provide a living example of how to face adversity with strength, determination, and courage.

Example: Laura grew up watching her mother and her friends, a tight-knit group of women, support each other through thick and thin. She recalls how her mother found strength in the unwavering support of her friends after losing her job; they encouraged her, helped her prepare for interviews, and celebrated every small victory with her. Inspired by their resilience, Laura carried this lesson into her adult friendships. When she faced a career setback, she leaned on her group of sisters as her mother had done.

This demonstration of resilience leaves an impression on younger generations. They learn that, even in difficult times, they are not alone. Instead, they are part of a legacy that values collective strength, the power of resilience and togetherness.

▶ Teaching Empathy And Compassion

Sisterhood fosters empathy and compassion, qualities essential for nurturing, healthy, and supportive, relationships. By showing kindness and understanding toward each other, we pass down the importance of emotional intelligence and being present for those we care about.

Jasmine shares how her mother and aunts taught her the power of empathy through their relationship with each other. They were each other's confidantes, listening without judgement and offering advice when needed. Watching them,

Jasmine learned that sisterhood was about shared experiences and understanding each other's emotions and challenges.

Now, Jasmine extends that same empathy to her friendships and family relationships, modelling the importance of truly being there for each other for her younger cousins. She encourages them to practice empathy in their interactions, fostering a generation of young women who prioritise understanding and compassion in their relationships.

▶ Creating A Safe Space For Vulnerability

One of the sisterhood's greatest gifts is the freedom to be vulnerable without fear of judgement. A sisterly bond can provide a rare space to share our insecurities, doubts, and fears in a world that often demands strength. Furthermore, this freedom to be vulnerable strengthens relationships and builds trust, making us feel genuinely seen and valued.

Lila and Maya, childhood friends who grew up as neighbours, have carried this openness into adulthood. Lila recalls a time when Maya confided in her about her struggles with anxiety, a topic they had not discussed before. Their bond grew more profound as they supported each other, sharing their fears and insecurities without hesitation. Over time, this relationship became a haven where both felt safe, to be completely honest.

When we model this openness for younger women, we demonstrate that true strength lies in authenticity. They learn that it is okay to be vulnerable and that a strong sisterhood will support them unconditionally. This lesson in trust and openness creates a legacy of relationships built on genuine connection and mutual understanding.

▶ Carrying Forward The Legacy Of Sisterhood

The bonds of sisterhood are a gift to be cherished and a responsibility to nurture. We leave an indelible mark on those who follow by passing down the values of loyalty, empathy, resilience, and joy. As each generation carries forward the lessons learned, they enrich the lives of the women around them, creating a ripple effect of love and support that transcends time.

Whether through traditions, guidance, or shared experiences, sisterhood as a legacy empowers women to embrace the strength of community. In our unique ways, we can pass down the gift of sisterhood by being there for each other, modelling compassion, and celebrating the power of women uplifting one another. This legacy will continue to flourish as long as we nurture it to become a source of inspiration and strength for future generations.

Sisterhood is a bond between women, whether biological or sisters by choice, built on love, trust, and understanding.

Murphy Browne

Murphy Browne is an African woman who was born in South America and grew up in an African-centred community where the elders told stories about their African ancestors and culture before the Maafa (African Holocaust.) Her elders were Pan-Africanists, greatly influencing every area of her life and informing her activism storytelling. Murphy is an educator, historian, and storyteller and writes a regular column for Share newspaper, also published online. She hosts two weekly radio programs at radioregent.com and is retired as an African Heritage Instructor with the Toronto Board of Education and the Toronto District School Board. She is a former Organization of Parents of Black Children member and the Black Action Defense Committee.

She is an active blogger at Words From Murphy Browne and published Berbiciangriot in 2015.

4

SISTERS

What or who is a sister? We have seen images of sisters on television programs and read about them in stories. We are sisters, and we have sisters. Sisterhood is a bond between women, whether biological or sisters by choice, built on love, trust, and understanding. A sister can be a biological sister, best friend, or member of the same religion or sorority. A sister will always be there for you in good times and not-so-good times. She truly knows and understands you. I grew up in a household with three biological sisters. There is something about a sister-to-sister bond that will never break.

Friends may come and go through different stages of life, but sisters are there forever. It is most likely cultural because I have read of biological sisters in some cultures who let go of each other because of a disagreement. The bond between my sisters and me is that we are related by blood. We, at times, only had each other to depend on, especially during our childhood. The nature of our father's employment (moving house to various parts of the country every two to three years whenever his employers directed) meant that it was often difficult to form friendships outside of the family unit.

In our family, whenever my father received a transfer, we packed our bags and moved to the place of the new posting. Although my mother lamented the inevitable broken dishes or furniture that resulted from each move, we did! So many moves did not facilitate lasting friendships, so we were each other's best friends for many years. We spent so much time together; we had to like each other to survive. Liking is as important as loving. We understand each other without ever having to explain ourselves. When one of us accomplishes something, we all share pride and glory. Sisterhood is the ultimate friendship that lasts a lifetime, a bond that is deeply rooted in our culture and personal experiences, enriching our lives in countless ways.

Our sister bond nurtured by our parents decades ago still binds us together. A 2009 study by a professor from the Psychology Research Institute of the University of Ulster found that having good relationships with your sisters is essential to your mental health. Psychology professor Dr. Tony Cassidy and his team tested the emotional well-being of 571 people aged seventeen to twenty-five. Some had only sisters or brothers, some had both, and others were only children. They found that those with at least one sister were more optimistic, less stressed, and better at coping with life's troubles.

Cassidy explained their findings: "We explain that the presence of girls opens up communication channels, and it becomes a much more expressive situation, and that's positive. Emotional expression is fundamental to good psychological health, and having sisters promotes this in families."

The researchers found that both men and women benefitted from having sisters, whether they grew up in a two-parent or single-parent home. Cassidy presented the study's findings at the British Psychological Society Annual Conference in Brighton, United Kingdom (UK) on April 2, 2009.

In her 1996 publication "No Friend Like A Sister: A Celebration in Words and Memories," Barbara Alpert wrote: "She is your mirror, shining back at you with a world of possibilities. She is your witness, who sees you at your worst and best and loves you anyway. She is your partner in crime, your midnight companion, someone who knows when you are smiling, even in the dark. She is your personal defence attorney and even your "shrink." Some days, she's why you wish you were an only child." This quote speaks to the love between biological sisters whose bond can sometimes be complicated.

When I think about sisters, I think of a song popular on the radio during my childhood in which the word "sister" was repeated. I vaguely remember the song and reached out to an elderly relative who remembered the lyrics. The song Sisters debuted decades ago in a movie I had never heard of: White Christmas.

"Sisters, sisters

There were never such devoted sisters

Never had to have a chaperone, no sir

I'm here to keep my eye on her

Caring, sharing

Every little thing that we are wearing

When a particular gentleman arrived from Rome

She wore the dress, and I stayed home

All kinds of weather

We stick together

The same in the rain or sun

Two different faces

But in tight places

We think, and we act as one - haha

Those who've seen us

Know that not a thing could come between us

Many men have tried to split us up, but no one can

Lord help the mister

Who comes between me and my sister

And lord help the sister who comes between me and my man. Sisters,

Sisters."

Hilarious but true for many who grew up in Guyana in the 1960s and 1970s. Listening to my relative sing that song, I reminisced about growing up with three sisters, especially one only a year and four months younger than I am. Our experience, in many ways, mirrored the sentiments expressed in the song.

I am thankful that I grew up in a home with three sisters (and several brothers). Although I respect the expertise of psychologists, I also value the experience of growing up with my brothers. I am sure that their presence contributed to my "good psychological health" and healthy self-esteem.

There is also the sisterly bond and love between chosen sisters. In her foreword to the book, "Comrade Sisters: Women of the Black Panther Party," activist and author Angela Davis noted that 66% of the membership of the Black Panthers was female. She writes: "Because the media focused on what could be easily sensationalized… There has been a tendency to forget that the organizing work that made the Black Panther Party relevant to a new era of liberation struggle rested on women's activities." The women of the Black Panther Party were sisters who worked together for a common cause. Even though they were not biological sisters, they chose to be sisters.

Sisterhood organisations that are part of North American culture include sororities. A sorority sister is a female college or university student who is a member of a social organisation exclusive to women. Many African American sororities started as a support system for African American women who attended post-secondary institutions and often were sometimes ostracised because of their gender and race. The term "sorority" comes from the Latin word "sororitas," which means "sisterhood" or "of or about sisters."

Sisterhood in sororities is vital in African American colleges and universities because it provides support and a sense of belonging. Sororities offer a safe space where women can feel accepted and where they can count on each other for support. Often, women created the sororities on principles of sisterhood, community service, academic achievement, and social development. Sororities provide lifelong friendships, educational support, service opportunities, and close-knit communities.

Sisterhoods in sororities can empower women to love themselves, grow, and learn more about themselves and their history as they grapple with a new phase of life. Sorority members have helped improve the quality of life in communities, alleviating poverty and illiteracy and fighting for justice. African American sororities have supported members in becoming better professionals in various fields. Sororities, a crucial system for African American women, also support mentoring and networking.

Sisterhood is essential to our survival in the 21st century as we contend with climate change and support the "Me Too Movement" and "Black Lives Matter" to protect future generations. Our foremothers experienced enslavement, and our version of freedom past the "International Decade for People of African Descent" (2015-2024) is different.

So, the notion of Sisterhood has always been encoded with a specific set of acceptance criteria that I never expected to achieve as a child.

Audra Townsend

Audra Townsend is a free-spirited British-born Jamaican-Canadian Data Privacy Specialist and abstract and mixed-media artist based in Toronto, Ontario.

As Director and founder of Audra 3.0 Inc., Audra's management consulting firm, she has provided privacy support for the work of Ontario's Digital First strategy and Digital First for Health strategy.

Audra is a self-taught artist and a trained Sociocultural Anthropologist who believes that, as humans, art is a manifestation of our curiosity about the material world and, as such, an essential part of what it means to be human. She borrows from intuitive and tactile (abstract) art forms to explore this relationship between art and the human experience. Her work characterizes a dense network of crisscrossing (and squiggly) lines separating rectangles of multiple shapes, made of different materials, earthy and celestial colours and textures from her use of materials such as sand, stone and, recently, Shin Noodle packaging.

She holds an MA in Anthropological Research from the University of Manchester in England and honours degrees in Social-Cultural Anthropology and Business Studies from York University in Toronto. Audra's artwork has been in exhibitions in Brussels, Halton/Georgetown, Madrid, Seoul, Toronto, and Vancouver.

5

GOING AGAINST THE GRAIN OF THE IDEA OF SISTERHOOD

The Universal Impact and Message Of Maya Angelou

When I think of Sisterhood, I reflect on the memories triggered by an old black-and-white 1972 photograph of my sister, our friends, and I lined up outside our apartment in Manchester, England. We ranged in age from three to seven and had our arms defiantly crossed over our little pudgy tummies. Our similar short white dresses signified we were all in tune with the popular culture of the 1970s, or perhaps some of our parents were the ones in tune with the popular culture of the time.

Paradoxically, I remember that even back then, my sister and I were not necessarily accepted as part of any group, let alone a Sisterhood. At home, especially on Saturdays, we did not receive the same care or attention as the other little girls. My sister and I were the only girls in the photograph not wearing the massive ribbons adorning our heads. Someone could ask the question, was our hair even combed? My mother's day off was Saturday, so she rarely combed our hair.

Those cunning little girls always ensured we knew they noticed these things about us. Their treatment of us manifested in absent or lost birthday party invitations or not inviting us to their homes to play. So, the notion of Sisterhood had a specific set of acceptance criteria that I never expected to achieve as a child, then as a teen, and eventually, as an adult.

Therefore, I go against the grain on any idea of a network of solidarity and support among women. I believe the notion, or even how it is applied, tricks women into thinking that disunity is unity and disempowerment is empowerment, as it intentionally excludes some women and, at a massive cost to society, reinforces group identity over the complexities of individual identity, experience, and belonging.

However, when I reflect on the women who are often excluded (the loners or overly independent), there seems to be an implied Sisterhood where membership is Guaranteed. It does not rely on an identifiable network of women and their individual experiences or accomplishments, and any woman is accepted to inspire everyone. To understand what I am talking about, one must reflect on one woman's universal impact and message, American poet and activist Maya Angelou.

First, the notion of Sisterhood often excludes women who do not fit into conventional norms or have similar backgrounds and life experiences. I know from personal experience and being a witness to someone else's pain. The idea leads to a profound alienation among those who feel they do not belong. Growing up, I remember my mother being alienated and excluded from the network of Jamaican and other Caribbean mothers that formed in our neighbourhood of the English working class and immigrants. My mother was viewed as an outcast because her personal choices and dislikes went against what brought the other mothers together.

She was not the mother known for her childcare skills, Jamaican/Caribbean cooking, or housekeeping. All of these things caused her anxiety and stress, so she was confused when performing them or avoided doing them altogether.

Our neighbours noticed, and they gossiped about it instead of being understanding or lending their support. This gossiping behaviour is unfortunate as supporting a woman in that crisis could have been unifying for those women while empowering my mother.

As a result of the treatment, my mother would feel inadequate and uncomfortable around those neighbours. At night, she would take refuge in a safe space among strangers of various backgrounds, which, at that time, was at the local Bingo for working-class and immigrant women in Manchester. I have to point out that my siblings and I were always excited when my mother went to Bingo. My maternal grandmother (who consequently did enjoy those things my mother disliked) often came over, or we went to her house. As a young child, with my grandmother present, home felt like a home, and the food was always fantastic.

One of my pet peeves is the Sisterhood's reinforcement of group identity over individuality. It does not only discourage individuality in women and girls. It crushes their spirit, particularly if they are having a bad day or life, making it difficult to achieve whatever criteria they need to meet to belong.

To some, this next issue may be trivial. However, I am concerned about certain ideals of femininity and beauty manifested within certain circles. It does not matter if the Sisterhood consists of Church Sisters, Work Sisters, or just friends. Our hair, make-up, nails, style of dress, and sometimes jewelry always seem to be key criteria in the acceptability of women among a group of women. I cringed when I heard the following from a group of women on the subway openly discussing and criticizing another woman. "What on earth is she wearing…what does she look like?"

This unity-disunity paradox makes many women extremely uncomfortable with individuality. If one disagrees with the opinions or ideas of the Sisterhood, it leads to conflict or avoidance-type behaviours. My siblings and I grew up as what is now called "overly independent children," so it is tough for us to either conform or pretend to conform to the norms or opinions of any group.

My eldest sister once told me that when she became a Christian, she silently prayed to Jesus because she did not want people to hear her say that He should not expect certain things from her because she would not do them. Women are frequently silenced, ostracised, or in trouble for acting outside the group's thinking, following their minds. Women accustomed to hearing the whispers from other women know what I am talking about. "Who does she think she is?"

As such, when I think of a Sisterhood as implied and universal, I think of Maya Angelou. Maya's all-knowing and in-your-face cheeky smile made her not only one of my favourite poets but one of my favourite women of all time. She was a genuine individual and change-maker who could speak a universally inclusive language that all women could understand. Indeed, Sisterhood and unity were the main themes in her poetry and prose.

However, the bonds that unite women in Maya's version of Sisterhood were acknowledging and understanding each other's hardships, struggles, differences, and pain. They were not what separated or divided us. They made our bonds even stronger.

As such, the personal message I take away from Maya's work is that all women are in a collective fight against oppression and that within itself should be the only criteria for being a member of the Sisterhood.

That message is why the following is my favourite Maya Angelou poem.

Still, I Rise

You may write me down in history
With your bitter, twisted lies,
You may trod me in the very dirt
But still, like dust, I'll rise.
Does my sassiness upset you?
Why are you beset with gloom?
'Cause I walk like I've got an oil well
Pumping in my living room.
Just like moons and like suns,
With the certainty of tides,
Just like hopes springing high,
Still, I'll rise.
Did you want to see me broken?
Bowed head and lowered eyes?
Shoulders falling like teardrops,
Weakened by my soulful cries?
Does my haughtiness offend you?
Don't you take it awful hard
'Cause I laugh like I've got gold mines
Diggin' in my own backyard.
You may shoot me with your words,
You may cut me with your eyes,
You may kill me with your hatefulness,
But still, like air, I'll rise.
Does my sexiness upset you?
Does it come as a surprise?

That I dance like I've got diamonds
At the meeting of my thighs?
Out of the huts of history's shame
I rise
Up from a past that's rooted in pain

I rise
I'm a black ocean, leaping and wide,
Welling and swelling I bear in the tide.
Leaving behind nights of terror and fear
I rise
Into a wondrously clear daybreak
I rise
Bringing the gifts that my ancestors gave me,
I am the dream and the hope of the enslaved person.
I rise
I rise
I rise.

Copyright Credit: Maya Angelou, Still I Rise from And Still I Rise:
A Book of Poems. Copyright © 1978 by Maya Angelou.

Sisterhood is more than friendship; it is an unbreakable bond between women. This bond connects us through compassion, empathy, and respect for one another,

Helen Pearman Ziral PhD

•••••••• ━━━━━━━━━━━━━━ ••••••••

Helen Pearman Ziral, PhD, is a professor, purpose-driven wellness coach, facilitator, and author passionate about forgiveness, personal transformation, and holistic wellness. She empowers women to embrace self-forgiveness, rediscover their true essence, and shine as authentic selves. Dr. Helen Z specializes in facilitating individual and group coaching sessions and leading transformative workshops focused on achieving balance across multiple dimensions of wellness. Her work inspires meaningful change and fosters lasting well-being.

•••••••• ━━━━━━━━━━━━━━ ••••••••

6

DEFINING SISTERHOOD

Sisterhood is more than friendship; it is an unbreakable bond between women. The bond connects us through compassion, empathy, respect for one another, and love. It's about connecting more deeply through understanding and support despite our differences.

A less formal yet robust description would include close-knit friends whose relationships are like family bonds—sometimes called "ride-or-die" circles. These circles act as sounding boards when facing tough decisions and offer camaraderie over wine nights or group chats when celebrating each other's achievements and everyday experiences.
Older generations may sometimes lean towards religious affiliations or spiritual practices, such as communal worship or prayer sessions. They sometimes build traditions among

followers, cultivating lifelong friendships based on shared values despite inherent cultural differences.

The following is my definition of sisterhood/sistering, along with suggestions and a discussion on strengthening the bonds between the fantastic women in our lives.

▶ S - Support unconditionally

Supporting our sister friends does not merely involve providing material items. Instead, when they experience challenging times, we should pause to walk alongside them, hold space, and offer emotional support, unconditional love, and a listening ear.

Sisterhood should prompt us to be excited about our sisters' significant accomplishments, whether job promotion, tenth work anniversary celebration, engagement, marriage, or addition to the family unit. Working women celebrate milestones such as these, demonstrating their perseverance. So, do not hesitate to look for opportunities to acclaim your sisters. Together, we can share their success stories (cheering/sending congratulations), celebrate birthdays, and organise parties or simple at-home events, which work better because of current economic situations.

▶ I – Inspire

I believe every woman has something unique and powerful within themselves. Based on this, I have cultivated mentorship relationships where I can offer guidance and inspiration to younger sisters centred around academic and career development.

▶ S – Stimulate and Support

We can promote and stimulate self-discovery, growth, development, and self-love through conversations and wisdom-sharing sessions.

Since we cannot avoid life challenges, whether big (e.g., divorce) or small (daily struggles, etc.), while working towards achieving our goals, we often seek encouragement during these overwhelming times when we mutter, "Just can't do this anymore!" That is where sistering support and inspiration come in. When women support each other, they become advocates for change.

▶ T – Trust

Sisterhood thrives on honesty, trust, and support rooted in accepting each other without hiding aspects of ourselves behind a veneer. The mask creates a disconnection from the bond we seek. Remaining honest and supportive in an environment of unconditional liking and love will strengthen sistering bonds.

▶ E – Empower

One hundred percent of female empowerment results in innovative solutions based on knowledge acquired through experience built on unending development. That can sometimes ignite an unbridled drive regardless of religion, culture, or social background.

▶ R – Reach Out and Respect Boundaries

Communication strengthens bonds. Regularly contact female family members or friends. Find out what they have been up to and discuss issues they are dealing with.

When interacting with sisters, consider boundaries and respect signals and red flags encountered. While persuasive techniques are often regarded as excellent energy boosters, enabling people to see a sister's vulnerability can foster effective communication.

▶ H – History of Sisterhood

Early in the 20th century, organisations such as suffrage and temperance played a significant role in inspiring sisterhood and promoting social causes. The most influential were women's clubs and The National Association of Colored Women, established in the late 1890s by African American women leaders. This organisation included women such as Mary Church Terrell and Harriet Tubman. Their activism paved the way for more excellent representation and empowerment of women in politics, education, and public service.

▶ O - Organisation

Organisation can play a critical role in forming healthy relationships. It fosters an environment where sisters are free to share differences of opinion. Dialogue and effective listening are encouraged in such a setting, engaging others and contributing positively to sisterly interactions.

▶ O – Opportunities

Sisters tend to embrace opportunities for volunteering and networking. When gathering around the metaphorical table, there is no limit to the number of people they may encounter. Volunteering creates a sense of community among sisters to help each other thrive.

▶ D – Diversity of cultures, education, and experience

Diversity of cultures, education, and experience demands that we recognise that the traditional notion of sisterhood might bring visions of giggly females running amok, sharing updates on their recent beau, and other cutesy stuff. However, sisterhood encompasses so much more. Sisterhood speaks to the female in the kitchen, operating room, classroom, boardroom, battlefield, political arena, or outer space. We are dissimilar, yet at our core, we are the same. We are strong, often resilient individuals capable of lifting each other as we manage topics ranging from financial wellness to interpersonal empowerment skills.

▶ Shared experiences

Whether visiting new places or experiencing unique moments, creating shared memories with another sister (the woman in your life) is essential. It strengthens bonds and helps sisters develop deeper connections with each other.

We connect with like-minded sisters in countless ways through various groups or communities. From women's clubs and organisations to sororities or online chat groups, finding an empowering network of females can lead to growth, healing, and personal fulfillment.

Sisterhood is a bond that connects women so strongly that it provides an energy boost that empowers them. However, the depth and strength are limited by how much effort goes into nurturing it through simple acts. Others may benefit by reaching out, collaborating, volunteering, celebrating achievements, and enjoying small moments together. These practices fuel lightweight but impactful inspirations.

The strong bonds built among women affirm that creating lifelong relationships takes time, effort, and patience beyond material gain. Knowing what to emphasise while establishing a relationship is important. Sistering is essential and can prove worthwhile in modern-day society, where strong female friendships encourage positive growth.

Sisterhood brings together women from different walks of life who share a common bond – women who believe in empowering each other while living inspired lives full of hope, gratitude, and joyfulness.

▶ Personal Growth

Sisters can access mentors who inspire and teach valuable skills and strategies for advancing career and lifelong goals at sistering events, whether workshops or online webinars.

Today, with the rise of social media and technology, millennial women have been fortunate enough to reap the benefits of online sisterhood. Digital communities can sustain global connections. Often, these platforms promote self-care through wellness-related activities like meditation, affirmations, or reading. At other times, they serve as support systems where geographical boundaries do not limit you.

Regardless of the female companionship and iteration one falls into, it is essential to remember that sisterhood is ever-evolving. Sometimes, sistering shifts over time based on personal interests or changes, so be open-minded and discover different configurations that best suit your needs. It is imperative to take action to nurture those connections further.

Sisterhood is a force for positive change when utilised effectively. Embracing various iterations and the bonding of sisters creates valuable networks promoting professional or personal growth, reinforcing values/principles across lifestyles and thereby creating lasting impact overall. Sisters everywhere are encouraged to embrace whatever resonates most today and tomorrow and not be afraid to explore new possibilities while being grateful for current ones already formed.

Sisterhood is about lifting each other, celebrating our unique strengths, and supporting one another through life's ups and downs. As a professor and expert in personal development and women's empowerment, I have seen firsthand the incredible impact a female connection can have on our well-being and success. Through sisterhood inspiration, we can tap into our potential and achieve greater happiness in our personal and professional lives. With strong sistering bonds, let us always remember to lift each other rather than tear each other down.

I grew up when learning from elders was not just expected but revered.

Rita Burke

Rita Burke's life story reflects a dynamic blend of cultural heritage, intellectual pursuit, and a commitment to service. Born and raised in Guyana, Rita's mother influenced her. She was a self-educated creative genius with a knack for turning limited resources into significant opportunities. This early influence laid the foundation for Rita's later achievements.

After completing her formal education, Rita worked as a secondary school teacher before relocating to England to pursue studies in healthcare. There, she met and married Sam Burke, and they moved to Toronto in the early 1970s. Rita continued her academic journey in Toronto, earning degrees in sociology, Caribbean studies, and education. Her professional career evolved as she worked as a Registered Nurse in several Toronto hospitals, later transitioning into a second career as an adult health care educator.

Rita's most significant academic accomplishment was her unexpected acceptance of a Nursing Professorship at Fleming College in Peterborough, Ontario. There, she co-authored the Trent-Fleming Nursing Degree Program, a part of the nursing curriculum today.

1994, Rita and Sam opened Burke's Bookstore, an Afro-centric resource hub. The bookstore, which focused on literature celebrating African culture and identity, has since transitioned into an online business, I Like Being Me Books.

Rita is also an accomplished author. She has co-authored four children's books with Sam and is working on her sixth. Her writing and contributions to education are deeply informed by her upbringing in a family of six sisters and her lifelong relationships with women worldwide, mainly her focus on sisterhood.

Her story concerns continuous learning, cultural pride, and a strong commitment to fostering connections and empowering others through education and literature.

7

AH! SISTERHOOD

Sisterhood is a sacred sanctuary where Black women can remove their shoes, let their hair down, laugh as loud as they want, and cry as often as needed. It is a place where we can unapologetically be free, unfiltered, and whole. Sisterhood is about camaraderie, power, empowerment, and collective tenacity. It is about holding each other up, lifting each other to new heights, and sharing the triumphs and struggles shaping our journeys.

I count it a privilege and an honour to have grown up in a home and community overflowing with the spirit of sisterhood. There were seven sisters — each beautiful, bold, and brilliant in her unique way. Some pursued formal education, while others embraced life's lessons, latching onto wisdom from our parents, family members, and the community elders who nurtured us. I grew up when learning from elders was revered, and the legacies and teachings bequeathed with intention and care. These elders, particularly the women, were the living embodiment of wisdom and knowledge, guiding us through the trials of life while instilling in us the values of strength, grace, and unwavering purpose.

The women educators I encountered in my formative years were knowledgeable, kind, insightful, fair, and generous. They modelled the behaviours expected from the young women in their care— showing us the power of self-respect, discipline, and intellectual curiosity. One of the most influential women in my life was Magda Pollard, the principal at my all-girls secondary school. Ms. Pollard was a leader who directed the all-female staff like the conductor of an established and professional choir.

Her leadership was a masterclass in organisation, vision, and care. She set high expectations for the young women who attended that school. While she recognised the importance of academics, she also demonstrated her keen understanding that a holistic education would prepare us for life beyond the classroom. With this in mind, she designed a curriculum that communicated through every lesson, every conversation, and every interaction that we were worthy, deserving, and able.

She was beautiful from my young, easily impressed mind— bold, brilliant, and unapologetically herself. She and many other women at that school became the role models I aspired to emulate. They inspired us to be our best selves, to set high goals, and how to achieve them. These women demonstrated that intelligence, beauty, and strength could coexist in the same person and that nothing could stand in the way of our success as long as we remained focused and determined.

Not once during my formative years or as a young adult did I feel that my melanated hue would prevent me from having a successful life. All the women I saw—whether at the elementary or post-secondary level—were brilliant, established, and thriving in their respective careers. Their examples made me believe that I could do the same. Our parents, too, instilled in us a resolute sense of self-worth. From the beginning, they taught us that we were strong enough, resilient enough, and bold enough. We were brave enough to face the world and all it held. And face it, we did—with boundless zeal, unyielding determination, and an infectious zest for life.

We did not have the language at the time to articulate it, but we embodied a deep sense of purpose and strength that uplifted one another. We lived out the words of Toni Morrison: "If you are free, you need to free somebody else. If you have some power, your job is to empower somebody else." This principle was the cornerstone of the sisterhood I experienced. Whenever one of us succeeded, it was a victory for all of us. Whenever one of us struggled, we were there to offer our support and to help her find her way. This spirit of solidarity was ingrained in everything we did and extended beyond the walls of our homes and schools.

Upon reflection, I now realise that what I experienced as a young woman was a sisterhood personified. When I needed my first job, my eldest sister, who worked at a hardware company, arranged my interview. Later, when I needed a second job in secondary school, my second eldest sister used her connections to make it happen. These acts of love and support were not only about providing opportunities—they were about ensuring that I knew I was never alone, that there were always women around me who wanted only the best for me, who were rooting for my success, and who would go out of their way to make sure I had what I needed to thrive.

As I spread my wings beyond my family, life gave me incredible women who became my sisters—not by blood, but by their kindness, generosity, encouragement, and foresight. I have come to understand that Sisterhood cannot be manufactured or designed. It is organic and dynamic, built on mutual respect, shared experiences, and a strong desire to uplift one another. It is felt, seen, and touched in the quiet moments of shared laughter, the late-night conversations about dreams and fears, the collective joy at each other's victories, and the steadfast support during times of struggle.

Ah, Sisterhood!

To the Black women who have shaped my life as far back as memory allows—I see, hear, feel, and celebrate you. I remember watching you in your uniforms, cycling to school, singing popular songs. You studied tirelessly for exams, pursuing that piece of paper that would ultimately pave the way for success in a world that was and still is all too ready to stack walls and hurdles against you. You never stopped fighting for your place in this world, and your strength and perseverance continue to inspire me today.

And when you dressed up—oh, the beauty! Your colourful dresses and hairstyles, inspired by Essence and Ebony magazines, were a testament to African elegance, boldness, and an indomitable spirit. You gracefully navigated the twists and turns of adulthood, finding jobs, forming families, and travelling to distant lands for further education. Through it all, a sister was always lifting and mentoring another, reminding us that we were never alone. There was always a sister to balance my life's challenges with joy, laughter, and an unspoken understanding of our shared perseverance and determination to advance.

Ah, sisterhood!

Moving to England brought me a new tribe of sisters—from Ghana, Nigeria, Jamaica, Trinidad, St. Lucia, St. Vincent, Barbados, and beyond. While studying at the same school and living under one roof, we transcended cultural differences to form a bond celebrating our individual and collective Africanness. We stood firm in relentless challenges, building a community rich in joy, friendship, and excellence. We were no longer just Black women from different parts of the world; we were sisters who shared a common history, ordinary everyday lives, and common triumphs.

Canada introduced me to another band of women kin. In churches, workplaces, and community groups, I found Black women from diverse backgrounds—those whose families had been here for generations, those who had come directly from the continent, and those with roots in the Caribbean. Together, we became nurturers, advocates, educators, and protectors—

bending like coconut trees in a storm yet refusing to be broken by a system designed to oppress us.

I saw the need for and created a book club in Peterborough for my melanated sisters. Initially focused on reading books that told our stories, the group quickly evolved into a quasi-support group—a san—in this sanctuary, shared soul-stirring, race-based, and job-related experiences. It became a haven where we could shed the masks we wore in public and be our authentic selves. We shared parenting tips, health and well-being tips, and strategies for navigating microaggressions and systemic racism. Reflecting on those enlightening years in Peterborough, I vividly recall the power of Sisterhood. What we did for each other through genuine love, care, and unconditional support was like the North Star guiding us through the darkest nights.

Despite the barriers, we excelled in our respective careers, kept our families strong, and thrived together. Sisterhood is woven into our lives and never ceases to be a powerful force that uplifts and inspires us. Like a snowstorm, our collective strength became an unstoppable force—challenges and all.

Ah, sisterhood!

Much like the days of our enslaved ancestors, Black women have always formed tight-knit bonds rooted in our ancestral ways of knowing, being, and existing. This spirit has given us richness and direction, enabling us to rise, overcome, and thrive beyond system-imposed odds. To my sisters everywhere—I see, hear, and feel you. Remember that we are standing on the shoulders of amazing Black women like Viola Desmond, Harriet Tubman, Rosemary Brown, Winnie Mandela, Ann Cools, and Toni Morrison, who faced challenges but remained steadfast. For these women, Sisterhood was an act of resistance. Our kinship, too, without labels, is an act of resistance and solidarity.

Remember, the strength of our ancestors has brought us this far, and we are, therefore, emboldened for the rest of the journey. Let us visualise ourselves standing on a foundation rooted in hope, optimism, and unyielding perseverance—values we must pass on to future generations.

Ah, sisterhood!

"Miss Patsy was always thrilled to see Kathleen. She loved how the young girl quickly settled into calling her Miss P, and of course, she relished her cooking."

Herma Killingbeck

Herma Killingbeck was born in Jamaica and moved to Canada at twelve. Proudly identifying as Jamaican-Canadian, she built a successful career in the corporate world before taking early retirement to pursue her first loves: reading, writing, and exploring the magic of words.

Herma's writing delves deeply into the profound question of what is lost and gained when people, often for economic reasons, leave behind the familiar to start anew in a foreign land. Through her stories, she seeks to give voice to the unique experiences of individuals, particularly those from the Caribbean diaspora.

Herma works part-time at a non-profit organization, continuing her journey of blending creativity with meaningful engagement in her community.

8

SUNDAY DINNER

Kathleen jumped up quickly, taking the plate with the crushed chicken bones from the older woman's hands, "Nope, you sit down. I'm on clean-up duty." The woman with the salt and pepper hair pulled back in a bun hesitated momentarily, shooting Kathleen a look of defiance that quickly dissolved into acquiescence as she handed over the plate and sat down, shifting until her body felt settled and fully contained in the chair. Loosely crossing her hands over her stomach, she sighed, satisfied. "Awright, thank you, mi dear". It was just the two of them again for Sunday dinner, a third-place setting remaining untouched.

As usual, cleaning up was easy. Miss Patsy kept the kitchen clean and organized even while preparing Sunday dinner, so Kathleen had it easy and was done quickly.

"Miss P, you ready for Mr. Bailey?" she called out as she emptied an ice tray into a small bucket. Not waiting for the answer she knew was coming, Kathleen grabbed the bottle from the corner shelf and two-stepped her way back to the dining table. "Wi need some Mr. Redding today," the older woman said as Kathleen made her way to the stereo, selecting the third album on the stand. Carefully pulling the vinyl from the cover, she placed it on the turntable and gingerly brought the needle over. The volume was just right, with the music there to encourage, soothe, or bridge any gaps in their conversation.

Taking her seat next to Miss P, Kathleen added ice to each glass, pouring just enough Bailey's to get them started and warrant a second pouring. They clinked glasses, smiling at each other warmly, "Cheers mi love." "To you, Miss P". They took a first drink and sat back, welcoming the warm sensation as the liquid and the music moved through their bodies. "Katti, mi did tell you bout the time mi almost go a Spain?"

Kathleen met Miss P during her second year of university, shortly after meeting Michael, her only child. He invited her home for Saturday soup before going out to the movies. Kathleen was living on campus then, rarely going home on the weekends, and immediately bonded with Miss P. Sitting at the small kitchen table drinking soup took Kathleen back to her early days with Miss Emmy and her childhood friend Joy.

Miss Patsy was always thrilled to see Kathleen. She loved how the young girl quickly settled into calling her Miss P and, of course, how she relished her cooking. "The last girl Michael bring 'ere, neva like fi eat. Mi nuh know if a mi food or wha. When mi offer her sumting, she seh "No, thank you".

Michael and Kathleen drifted from friends to lovers and gradually back to friends with no drama. The relationship took them along for a ride, and then they parked where it was supposed to be. The women found themselves missing each other. Kathleen kept her distance, not wanting to make things uncomfortable for Michael's new girlfriend. Every so often, though, Michael would deliver a care package from his mother. "She told me…Tek dis for Katti, yuh know how she luv mi cooking."

Eventually, Michael and Kathleen got their degrees and jobs. Kathleen started sharing an apartment with her friend Jacqueline. She rarely saw Michael, so she called Miss P, telling herself it was to check on the older woman.

One evening, Kathleen was browsing at the mall. Going home meant she would either have to listen to Jacqueline and her boyfriend Matt being all lovey-dovey or console Jacqueline as she cried over their latest fight. She had nothing left for that today, not after the brutal day at work.

"No, I do not want another one. I would like to return this one, please, and thank you." She knew that voice, the precise pronunciation she used outside the home, and recognized the upright bearing. Kathleen resisted the impulse to rush to her, to fall into her arms, and instead waited off to the side, giving Miss P space to finish up with the sales lady. Then she saw what she hoped she would see: the biggest smile on Miss P's face as they hugged each other.

Against Miss P's protests, Kathleen drove her home and accepted her invitation to Sunday dinner. And so, it had started, Sundays with the young woman and the woman not quite old enough to be her grandmother but also not young enough to be her mother's cohort.

That first Sunday in the tidy apartment, Kathleen asked if Michael would be joining them since there were three place settings at the table. She had heard through the grapevine that he was on a secondment to New York. "We'll see, mi dear, we'll see. Mi just glad fi see yuh." Kathleen started to rely on these Sunday dinners to yearn for that feeling that coursed through her on Sunday nights.

Most people didn't know she had a family in Brampton, one with her mother, stepfather, younger brother, and sister. Kathleen was raised by her mother's aunt, Miss Emmy, since the age of three, when her mother, then twenty-one, left for Canada to make a better life for them both.

Kathleen joined the Hamiltons, as she called them, at age sixteen, which most people say is the right age to get used to the Canadian way and then go on to university. Her new family did their utmost to make Kathleen feel included, but she always felt like the odd piece that did not belong. Now, she was sure they did not miss her absence; she had graduated and made a life for herself, so they no longer had her as a responsibility.

Every Sunday, as she turned the door handle, the plastic on the settees, the crocheted doilies on the coffee table, the "welcome mi dear," and the smell from the kitchen reached out to loosen the knots she carried in her body. At Miss P's home, Kathleen could rest her mind, lower her shoulders, and laugh out loud. She understood the language in this apartment, the words said and unsaid. She was Miss Emmy's and Joy's Katti, not Kath, struggling to find her place in this foreign land.

"….but as mi madda used to seh, one-one coco full basket." Evelyn Maud Montague looked at the young woman curled up on the settee, eyes closed and snoring ever so slightly. She loved her like a daughter, worried about her, and felt protective of her. She thought about how different things were for her. "Not like when mi did come. Dat time, you have to batta, batta, find yuh way yuh self."

Those days, the world stretched out in front of Evelyn. She had left her little village and travelled far to this foreign land alone. She knew a few people, including Miss Lily's son Fred, Miss Ivy, and her husband Mas Tom. So yes, she had people to turn to if things got really bad, but you could not make things get that bad. She worked two jobs to pay her rent, save some money, and still send money home each month and a barrel for Christmas. She planned to start nursing school after saving enough, so she had little time or money for going out.

"One day, mi tek mi bright self and guh seh yes to Mr. Man and braps, next ting yuh know Michael come. Yes, mi did want to be a madda, but lawd, not on mi own. Mi always dream seh mi wudda

get married, buy a house and den hav wi children. Mi madda did want mi fi go weh, instead of stay home and hav pickney. When mi just come, mi did feel seh mi coulda tek life. Bwoy, it look like seh life tek me."

There was no regret for having Michael though. He was the apple of his mother's eye, big shot vice-president now. She wished she could see him more, though. He was talking about cruising to the Bahamas with his girlfriend's family instead of coming home for Christmas.

She caught her reflection in the window and, at that moment, saw flashes of the little girl playing in the river, the young woman saying goodbye to her parents, her dream of becoming a nurse, the transference of that dream to nurturing a bright little boy, and her almost trip to Spain.

Her gaze moved to the sleeping young woman. Earlier, when they greeted each other, the older woman was sure she felt pieces move in the young woman's body as they hugged. She held her a bit gentler, longer. In that space between dream and waking, the young woman returned to a time before she knew there was a feeling of not being whole.

The HashTags become a digital blanket wrapping me in a hug of support and encouragement

Nancy Fraser

Nancy Fraser is a college professor whose work focuses on the intersection of race, gender, and education, particularly within Caribbean families. Her favorite quote is: "If you are silent about your pain, they'll kill you and say you enjoyed it." Zora Neale Hurston

9

HASHTAG SOUL SCRIBBLES

A day in the Life of Black Sisterhood Online

The muted ping on my phone and the soft light filling the room pull me into a new day. It's 7:10 AM on Friday, and surprise, surprise, I've overslept again. I need to be at work by 9, but before I dive into the chaos, let's check in on the sisterhood. Since joining a few Black women's groups on social media, scrolling through my feeds has become a morning ritual. Within seconds, I'm laughing out loud and fully awake. 'Goddess' writes, "My Nana makes the best potato salad, y'all!!! #MyNanaIsBetterThanYours #BlessedNHighlyFlavored #NoRaisins." The highly flavoured part has me cracking up. My Black sisters know how to turn anything into a hashtag. With one eye on the clock, I quickly scroll through my usual feeds, hunting for more gems under #MelaninPoppin, #BlackExcellence, and #BlackGirlMagic.

I arrive at work with minutes to spare, balancing my Stanley Cup, a box of Timbits, and a low-key anxiety that's becoming a norm. As I place my cup on the desk, I see another card. The fifth one this month. This one features two brown bears embracing on the cover. Sweet, but a little on the nose. Inside, the now familiar script reads, "This too shall pass. God needed another angel. Always here for you." Grief language? Without a doubt. Platitudes? Maybe. For the rest of the morning, the card has successfully wormed into my thoughts and taken up space. What do people mean when they say, "This too shall pass"?

Later, scrolling through the digital halls of one of my favourite online Sisterhood communities, I stumble upon a post that validates my grief, not as something that is passing, in a here-today-gone-tomorrow type thing. The post, reflecting on grief and loss, features a Toni Morrison gem: "I want to feel what I feel, even if it's not happiness." #Word! This, right here! This is a line that reverberates. I want to feel my pain, my despair, my confusion, my sorrow, my loss.

By lunchtime, my feed has shifted to reflect the rhythm of a woman's working day. Hashtags like #WomanEmpoweringWomen and #Sisterhood dominate my timeline, with each story demanding my attention. The hashtags become a digital blanket, wrapping me with support and encouragement. One poster shares safety tips for women of rideshare vehicles, and she ended it with #NotTodayKidnappers and #RideOrDieButMostlyRide. It's one of those moments where a smile tugs at the corners of your mouth because of its humour and hard facts, but the tragedy of how necessary these tips are hit deeper than any clever hashtag.

Another post tells the story of a young woman who shattered the glass ceiling at a male-dominated company. She shares her journey to find the confidence to lead men who were already certain she would fail and had no problem being vocal about it. I scroll through the outpouring of responses from many women in this digital space, and it feels like a good ole, warm, collective hug. I can't help but linger a while on this story, reading all the comments where women share not only their solidarity but their sadness, their anger, and their hope for a world where people see and hear women so they feel empowered to create and be in spaces where their contributions are valuable and essential. #WomenInLeadershipMatter #Period!

After a long day's work, I'm finally home, feet up, wrapped in the warmth of a steaming cup of cocoa tea. My scalp still tingles from the deep conditioning of coconut and peppermint oil I indulged in.. It's a weekly ritual as much about hair care as it is about reclaiming time for myself. I am fully immersed in HairToc now, deep in the realm of my #NaturalHairJourney. Then, a post stops my scroll.

It's a short video on "tame" short, kinky hair to make it look "presentable" in a professional setting. There was a collective digital gasp. Wait, what? One woman asks the obvious: Why presentable? The comment section erupts in a conversation that is nothing short of liberating. "If my hair offends you, imagine what my confidence must do.

#AintBowingToEurocentricExpectations." Another woman chimes in, "It's wild how 'professional' is just code for 'less Black'. The energy is contagious. Before I know it, I am scrolling through my photos, looking for one to share because this crown of mine, now dusted with wisdom, deserves to be seen and celebrated, too. Maybe I'll tag it with #GreyCrownMagic.

As the day winds down and the sun sinks behind snow-capped trees, I begin my nightly routine. I finished the laundry, dinner was behind me, and the house, once filled with the familiar chatter of my children, was now quiet. With both away at college, the silence is something I'm still learning to sit with. I slip a bookmark into the pages of The Sisters Are Alright by Tamara Winfrey-Harris and reach out for my phone. Before I turn in, I need to feed my soul once again.

The posts on my feed now feel like a collective exhale. They are softer. Quieter. It is as if the diet is astral space itself, recognising that it's time to unwind. Maybe it's because it's Friday evening, the threshold of the sacred two-day ritual of spirit rejuvenation. One post shows a picture of a steaming bathtub decorated with wine and roses. It is a gentle reminder to put yourself first, tagged #SelfCareWeekend. Another feature is a woman journaling in a moonlit window, with the caption urging other women to show up as their true, authentic selves daily. I pause. I need this reminder, too. Some days, showing up for myself is the most radical thing I can do.

Scrolling through these posts can be heavy sometimes, but it's almost always grounding. These soul scribbles remind me that even when the world feels unbearable, we've built and maintained spaces to hold each other up. These digital sisterhoods are more than applications and platforms; they are soulful and vibrant sanctuaries. This deep, unspoken understanding extends beyond hashtags and mindfully assembled timelines because these spaces are curated by and for women, particularly Black women.

These online communities hold space for the joys, the struggles, the victories, and the vulnerabilities of Black womanhood and womanhood in general. Whether it's sharing a recipe, having a laugh together, uplifting and amplifying each other's voices, celebrating the wins, or offering comfort in moments of pain and sadness, the digital sisterhood transforms virtual interactions into tangible bonds. The connections are undeniably real. Here, distance does not weaken the connection; it amplifies it. These digital spaces remind Nancy that sisterly love and support do not need a physical room to flourish.

Community power exists, especially when its members pour into one another. Sisterhood thrives here, connected by bandwidths of resilience and creating a cyber haven where women from all walks of life are seen and celebrated. #MySoulScribbles.

❝

Of blood and kin I thee celebrate. The journey of love and friendship that we have been bonded throughout life's ups and downs.

Pauline Taylor-Bloomfield

The foundations of Sisterhood are laid during childhood, where sisters share a significant portion of their early lives.

Hermia Morton Anthony

$$\mathbf{66}$$

When we model our openness for younger women, we demonstrate that true strength lies in authenticity.

———

Asali Quamina

❝❝

Sisterhood is a bond between women, whether biological or sisters by choice, built on love, trust, and understanding.

———

Murphy Browne

❝

So, the notion of Sisterhood has always been encoded with a specific set of acceptance criteria that I never expected to achieve as a child.

———

Audra Townsend

❝

Sisterhood is more than friendship; it is an unbreakable bond between women. This bond connects us through compassion, empathy, and respect for one another,

Helen Pearman Ziral PhD

66

I grew up when learning from elders was not just expected but revered.

Rita Burke

❝

Miss Patsy was always thrilled to see Kathleen. She loved how the young girl quickly settled into calling her Miss P, and of course, she relished her cooking.

———

Herma Killingbeck

66

The HashTags become a digital blanket wrapping me in a hug of support and encouragement.

———————

Nancy Fraser